Finding Joy
in School Runs

Finding Joy in School Runs

Florence Ilumoka

Xulon Press

Xulon Press
2301 Lucien Way #415
Maitland, FL 32751
407.339.4217
www.xulonpress.com

© 2020 by Florence Ilumoka

All rights reserved solely by the author. The author guarantees all contents are original and do not infringe upon the legal rights of any other person or work. No part of this book may be reproduced in any form without the permission of the author. The views expressed in this book are not necessarily those of the publisher.

Printed in the United States of America.

ISBN-13: 978-1-631-29733-5

ACKNOWLEDGEMENTS

With God all things are possible, so finishing this book, publishing, and editing it is to the glory of God Almighty.

All thanks to God Almighty and to Him alone be all the glory.

Thanks to my lovely family for their support throughout the whole period of writing this book, especially my dearest husband Olusoji Ilumoka who has been incredibly supportive, always there and an absolute inspiration in achieving this goal.

My wonderful children (Yemidale, Temidire & Ayotide), for their uttermost support over the years on this journey about school runs for my book. I love you all and appreciate all your encouraging words.

Also, a big thank you to everyone, friends and family who have contributed in one way or another in making this book a success

CONTENTS

1. SET THE PACE FOR JOYFUL RUNS. 1
2. PREPARE FOR CONTINOUS EXICITEMENT. 5
3. LEARN TO BE PATIENT 7
4. BECOME MOTIVATED. 9
5. ENCOURAGE YOURSELF 11
6. CONFIDENCE ABOUT YOUR APPEARANCE 15
7. REMEMBER TO BE READY AND POSITIVE ABOUT THE DAY 17
8. REMIND YOURSELF ABOUT YOUR DREAM 19
9. ENJOY THE JOURNEY 21
10. AVOID THE BAD HABIT OF CHATTING FOR LONG 23
11. TAKE YOUR SCHOOL RUNS AS A SERIOUS JOB. 25
12. ALWAYS TRY TO MAKE PEACE OUT OF EVERY CHALLENGE 27
13. CONFIDENCE ABOUT TOMMORROW 29
14. SCHOOL RUNS SELF-AUDIT QUESTIONEER. 31

1. SET THE PACE FOR JOYFUL RUNS.

This book is all about parents and their children doing great things together during the dropping off and picking up from school on school days normally referred to as **"School runs"**, and the intensity of this activity focusing mainly on the children's happiness, all of which have turned many children helpers into self-involved and fragile conformists in the race of school runs.

Frankly speaking, it is really a joyful, wonderfully fulfilling and positively challenging job for parents who are willing to prepare well for it.

Looking critically at it, the rapid and widespread bonding routine of parents and children going through school runs has become more desirable than ever before, even as the population in schools continue to increase, resulting in a consequent increase in the population of those involved in school runs.

This is a positive development as the desire to get closer to each other is being strengthened through school runs. Apart from the immediate and apparent benefit of parents and children bonding, there are other long-term benefits that will help the children attain a more balanced ***psychological and physiological growth***, as well as overall wellbeing.

It can be reasonably argued that in the least, school runs can be perceived as a difficult, boring, and depressing daily routine or task if one is not tuned to experiencing it joyfully. However, our focus as parents or guardians should be the joy of witnessing and being a major contributor to the healthy development of our children and their eventual success in life. Our interactions with our children's teachers and the interactions of the teachers with our children are very crucial factors in building up or eroding the children's morale and self-esteem fabric in their life's journey.

School runs is therefore a profound activity which leaves an indelible mark as footprints in the minds of both parents and children. According to research, the presence of parents around their children gives them a reason to smile, which means a lot to the children. Although some days may not go or be as good as planned, there is always something good in each day, so partners and helpers should support one another during school run challenges. The joy expected from this activity called **'school runs'** is the positive future outcome of the whole running exercise, which more than makes up for the difficulties and challenges we face, particularly when we know that ***"nothing in life comes easy"***. So, the benefits associated with school runs can be clearly seen in the future ahead. This means that the

1.   SET THE PACE FOR JOYFUL RUNS.

challenging bits of it can be turned around and forged into joyful memories of a series of worthwhile and beneficial events.

As a parent myself, I understand the intensity of school runs and its challenges. I have been there and in it for a while, and I am still doing it. I realize that nothing great in life is ever achieved without much effort and enthusiasm. One must also emphasize the fact that positivity and enthusiasm are things of the mind, just like when you think happiness and you are happy within yourself no matter what you may be going through at that point in time, you just know that the **gloom is just temporary and not forever**; and before you know it, a light comes shining through. When one considers the positive attribute of school runs which lays huge emphasis on the children's happiness at the critical age they are in, then the main purpose of this activity which is to help them go through life with ease as they grow up, is achieved. The importance of this cannot be overemphasized, particularly when underscored by the fact that when you are optimistic in life, it acts as a magnetic tool to happiness, which then draws good things and good people to you.

Looking at the sacrifices we make for our children as parents to do school runs, the whole running activity stems from the desire for us to make our children become better or great in life. A key factor to achieving this is to do more of what makes you happy, because **when you think you are happy, you will be happy, simply meaning that something positive can always come out of a negative situation.**

Our main fixation in life is the future we focus on, so we should take pride and have faith in what we are doing, and do it well, and the result will be an amazing sense of fulfilment and joy at the end of the day.

2. PREPARE FOR CONTINOUS EXICITEMENT

To every child in school, the world is seen as an exciting place to be, but which could sometimes on the contrary, ***"be frightening and unpredictable."*** It would do a world of good to start your school run day with a decision to make it as exciting and memorable as you can in your getting ready by first freshening up to smell nice, then dressing up nicely and finally arming yourself with a forward looking and joyful program for the day. Your day may be filled with planning your route well, preparing your mind to be positive before and after, taking on some of your other daily routines which may include gardening, shopping, researching for your career or business, going to the gym or library, so don't just go home to do chores and watch television all morning.

FINDING JOY IN SCHOOL RUNS

You should be prepared to confront challenges without losing your positivity for the rest of the day. See your school run as a temporary phase for the greater good, and always be ready to quickly move forward from every unpleasant experience. Have a life and let the children in your care see you as human; **someone who is not just doing the runs as a burden, but as someone doing it with love.** It would not only help the children psychologically, it would also help them to focus and see school as *a place to go to,* learn at, and excel with joy. Just trust and believe that they would cherish every moment of joy that you put into the experience which gives great warmth and comfort to them, and this will make their attitude positive to everyone in school.

Such memorable years would provoke great confidence and courage in every child in school. No one wants any distance between them and their children, so school runs are a sacrifice we make for our children and it helps to enhance family bonding. Great warmth is achieved by fostering a loving relationship which is essential in the development of a child's brains as they grow up into adulthood. It is a long lasting emotional and physical tool in the healthy development that helps in shaping the future of the children.

3. LEARN TO BE PATIENT

The love and patience a mother contribute to a child's life can be likened to *"a tube of toothpaste that keeps on squirting toothpaste and never runs out of supply".* When you have patience in your life, it brings about humility in you. Being humble and being patient work hand in hand, and with that you will achieve a lot. No matter the situation you find yourself in, when you are patient you will be able to handle it.

To achieve the joy in school runs revolves around you being patient. Taking care of children can be tasking, but with patience and a decision to believe in God's help, you will be able to handle every situation. Going about your daily school run can be demanding, but when you look at it as something of joy, the tender care and happiness that permeates everywhere with school runs will also impact positively on the educational needs of the children. Educational needs revolve around the daily activities that is going on in the environment the children are in.

Talking to children about any tragic situation without scaring them is important. The way we present such situations should be such that it will not upset the children, and this should be done in a very tactful manner, devoid of fear. Safety skills is another important aspect that needs to be discussed with the children, and as a parent you will have to play along with them doing things together with them in order for them to learn and build up these skills. It is also useful to guide the children in the daily routine adopting a step by step approach towards learning these skills. Things like crossing the road safely should be done together, crossing at designated crossing points, and doing it several times in order to instill the habit in the children which will soon become a set pattern that everyone must follow in a joyful way.

Also important are navigating key landmarks, awareness of problems on the routes to school and how to make them streetwise to be more watchful or vigilant of any dangerous activity around them. The joy or happiness we derive as parents doing school runs should be a thing that is relished in with the children.

We need to lecture the children and encourage them to gain independence and confidence when they are on their own. Being independent and confident gives us rest of mind and confidence that our children can take care of themselves when on their own.

4. BECOME MOTIVATED

Being motivated doing school runs means being inspired to be joyful as a parent. To become a joyful parent is not so hard if we chose to be motivated with the responsibility that comes our way. It is not just about being contented with being a mother and a father and paying someone else to always do your school runs while you face other things in life. Whether you are a mother or father, or a guardian for that matter, you need to encourage yourself to continually develop your daily motivational attitude for a beautiful day by plugging into the morning energy routine if you are not sick or ill.

Network with trusted families and friends for emergencies if you are a single parent, and let your days be full of hope, fun and laughter. Do not be bugged down by negatives that have no immediate outcome when you have a school run duty at hand. Always see it as a 365-day experience meant for a period. During challenges or difficult situations, be loving and friendly to everyone in the simplest and nicest manner on your way to doing your school runs. Do not frown or carry the world on your shoulders as if you are the only one who has ever been is such a condition or situation.

Do your school runs as a part of your *"skill development experience in your business or career"*, because it is not just about dropping children or child off quickly at school, there are many other things involved.

It is a lot more about your human and emotional management of people and children on your school runs; people such as other parents, children, teachers, guardians, friends and the head teacher, all with their various backgrounds. It is your look, smile, attitude, kind words, composure, and consideration for peace that every child would learn from. Such efforts then become a benefit to you in the short and long run in terms of managing people from all walks of life. Being motivated in everything you do brings about joy and happiness, especially when you enjoy what you are doing. It then becomes easier to be *"an achiever in life either in your career or any other thing of interest."* The joy you derive from school runs revolves around you being motivated. When you are motivated it brings about the best in you, when you enjoy what you are doing, it will ultimately boost your morale.

5. ENCOURAGE YOURSELF

Encourage yourself to believe that school runs are a joyful activity that needs to be appreciated for a period. Always look forward to dropping off and picking the children by planning your time with some flexibility based on a variety of options and this would be helpful to both you and the children. Have reliable friends or helpers by making every effort to build friendly and responsible relationships with those having regard for safety. You should also safeguard all children in your care with that same level of trust and confidence you wish to see in anyone you entrust them to, because as responsible parents or guardians they would also look out for this trait in you.

FINDING JOY IN SCHOOL RUNS

The child, children and helper would see such joy and diligence in you and ensure that they play their own parts with joy and sincerity because they see the joy and happiness in you. It is in fact a ***"temporary unpaid job"*** for many parents who do school runs and are without a mainstream or temporary job. Having a break in your career, does not now mean that you are doomed to do school runs forever. It is only a means to an end and never an end, or the end of your career. Determine to do something about how you use your time productively during the gaps in your school runs.

Our main or primary motive in life as parents should be leaving "***a legacy of love*** "and a caring attitude for our children during and after school runs to enable them to become better people and great achievers. Sacrificing for your children is something that will live long in their memory. It can be depressing when you think of your career, your job and education being on hold because of your children. Avoid such morbid and negative thoughts and have a strong forward plan. "***The rewards of any personal joyful school run are memorable and ever green",*** and it is more than any return on investment that come from money given to the children or careers at some point another.

By motivating yourself, you do not think of school run as a difficult thing to do, but as a joyful activity for every parent and genuine guardian. Mothers are particularly naturally caring and with lots of understanding when it comes to ***"school runs"*** unlike fathers. Mothers have a soft spot in handling children well. Men cannot do it as well a woman do; so, school runs naturally turn out to be a task for women.

Most children tend to think of their mother as more caring because of the better bonding achieved during school runs, they feel more relaxed talking to mothers rather than their fathers. More so,

5. ENCOURAGE YOURSELF

whatever you want your child to be in life should be the effort of both parents, the guidance a child will need in life will always be the sacrifice you give them.

6. CONFIDENCE ABOUT YOUR APPEARANCE

Your appearance also really matters. Focusing on school children runs does not mean you should appear shabby.to be confident shows, you are sharp and approachable. When you go to drop off your child in school in the mornings or pick them up in the afternoon, dress well and smell nice. Look at school runs as a temporary work, away from your normal work. The way you present yourself speaks volume about you.

FINDING JOY IN SCHOOL RUNS

Caring for yourself is not a **"selfish act"**, it simply a combination of a good social, emotional, and physical health state. When you do not feel good about your own very self or are not making effort to dress the way you feel is ideal for you, it will constantly lead to low self-confidence or self-esteem.

When you appear looking well, people would like to talk to you, and you can even share some ideas with other parents. Being confident can be seen in you when you appear well, you do not need to say much.

Looking good makes you feel better within yourself and you can also then confidently compliment other parents that look well. Complimenting each other and encouraging each other can boost the morale of other parents that might be feeling down before. Enjoy every bit of the school run so that your children can be positive in life.

To overcome low self-confidence, you need to concentrate more on the successes you have in life and "***never dwell on failures but learn from them.***" The best way to overcome any negativity is to set a goal for yourself and focus on your true achievements so far, then remind yourself of how well you have done.

7. REMEMBER TO BE READY AND POSITIVE ABOUT THE DAY

When you have a career break, you can really feel down. Being a career-oriented person can make you feel down within yourself, but if you can see school runs as something joyful and for the progress or happiness of your children, then you will never feel down. With determination of steel, you can even build your career over a period and still be doing school runs. By engaging yourself with creative ideas, it can develop into something phenomenally successful. Another thing we should bear in mind is that "*school run is not forever*;" these children will grow up to a stage that we will not need to do school runs with them again. When you are confident and have the belief in yourself then you can do so many things.

FINDING JOY IN SCHOOL RUNS

As a career minded person, you can organize events during your spare time, go for exhibitions, invite other parents to different events and anything of interest. Benefiting from each other is a tool one can use to discover or re-discover oneself. You can even exchange ideas in different fields or skills and that will make you more confident in yourself and be more fulfilled at some point or another.

Cultivate the habits of being yourself, not wanting to be someone else. Believe in yourself, and do not see others as better than you or more deserving than you are. Look at yourself as being equal to everyone else. Being engaged in different activities makes you terribly busy and school runs will be a thing of joy and not a drawback. It even shows you how much you can still achieve during this period.

The joy of school runs can be achieved and appreciated when you are fully engaged in things you enjoy doing.

8. REMIND YOURSELF ABOUT YOUR DREAM

There is a reason for every season of school runs. Create a dynamic and exciting weekly goal that builds up to a final achievable smart goal. Something you like and you are passionate about that follows your daily school runs.

Being successful in life is through the choices we make, and we are the only person that can write or re-write our own destiny. Avoiding responsibility or blaming and pointing fingers will lead to making excuses for any failure or unsatisfactory life choices we make.

The most important thing in life as a parent doing school runs on a temporary basis, is knowing exactly the things that are important to us in life by prioritizing them.

FINDING JOY IN SCHOOL RUNS

We should analyze things and separate what is important to us from things that are not especially important. Our obligations as parents is to do what will be of benefit to us and our children that will make us happy.

"School runs are meant to be enjoyed and not for making excuses for not achieving certain things in life."

Doing school runs should make an impact in the life of your children, your actions or achievement are part of it all. Mistakes or failures makes us grow, and this does not amount to total failure in life. We can also keep learning, loving and at the same time living a good life by doing school runs. Movement in life is all about growth, deciding to change the way you do things and making new things happens in your life. Your daily attitude to get the best out of anything you are doing is an achievement to greater things to come in life.

"To be an achiever or a winner in whatever you do, you must have the ability to be optimistic." Optimistic people see any discomfort or failure as an avenue to grow and learn new lessons from life. Why not let us see the opportunity in school runs to learn, because the world is full of endless opportunities.

9. ENJOY THE JOURNEY

Any school run trip whether by car, foot, bus, or train can be very unnerving, so prepare yourself, and psyche yourself up for this temporary phase of your life.

One thing we should be aware of is that every day we grow stronger learning from our many struggles in life.

No doubt, life can be a struggle. It will break you down sometimes such that no one can protect you from it. Hiding alone in your own bubble or somewhere away from everyone else will not help either. Prolonged solitude will break you up with an endless thirst for friends and connection. **_Learn to love and live_** because it is the main reason we are here on earth.

FINDING JOY IN SCHOOL RUNS

Going through the stress of school runs can be something of a healthy guideline towards a positive change in life.

To achieve greater success especially with our children it requires our dedication and struggles before we can get there.

Sacrificing our time and career may sometime risk our wellbeing, and somehow, we may also sometimes be bruised by life. If this happens and you get hurt, betrayed or neglected, remember to reflect on all the good times you've had, all the sweetness you have ever tasted, and all that you have learned at different stages in life. So, it makes more sense to remind yourself how amazing it was to live and enjoy life.

Having not struggled for anything in life should never be considered a blessing. The only way to move forward in life is the discovery of oneself amidst the depths of despair in one's hour of darkness, when the light illuminates everything and despair fades away leading us to rejoice and enjoy the blessings of life.

10. AVOID THE BAD HABIT OF CHATTING FOR LONG

It is always tempting to have long chit chat with friends or family on Playgrounds.

Be focused on the positive side of things and be wise enough to walk away from any negativity or unproductive chatting.

Finding joy in school runs is enhanced by spending more of your time with the right people that make happiness their main priority in life no matter the situation.

Happiness and joy in doing school runs make life simpler and will help with limiting or letting go of one's selfish behaviors. Remember, you still have a lot of special things to offer to the world after school runs finishes. Why not build your life during school runs and be a better person after school runs is over?

FINDING JOY IN SCHOOL RUNS

We can make a difference in the world by starting with the world around us and making our children smile can make other people around them smile too. Your total engagement and focus on school runs will make a difference in your children's lives which can easily and naturally spread, having desired impact on others.

The best result in life can be seen when we smile more often because life is like a mirror, so let us do more of talking about positivity than negativity.

11. TAKE YOUR SCHOOL RUNS AS A SERIOUS JOB

Take your school runs seriously like you would take a 9am to 5pm job. Take time to prepare for and enjoy the day. Remove all your worries and stay focused. The ability to be successful in life is helped by being optimistic in anything you are doing; you can start a happy and successful business while doing school runs especially if it is something that relates to it.

One should make no room for failure to be successful in these stressful times. Failure should only be regarded as an opportunity to grow and turn things round to success. Most parents look at school runs as a trying time or stressful time, but we should see it as a time filled with endless opportunities and endeavor to be more optimistic and creative.

FINDING JOY IN SCHOOL RUNS

School runs makes us more focused and more aware of our environment, though it sometime feels like time is standing still, but the fact is when you are involved in a task that makes you more focused you will achieve a lot more in life.

Engaging in other productive activities and dedicating yourself to the task joyfully, psychologically equips you ahead of the daily routine. To a dedicated school runs parent, there are lots of preparation to embark upon which is meant to fully equip us for the task ahead. During this period magical things are likely to happen because you are extremely focused and in a positive state of mind and wellbeing.

12. ALWAYS TRY TO MAKE PEACE OUT OF EVERY CHALLENGE

One truth in life is that perfection is not static and cannot exist in a static state of mind because life is a continuous journey, constantly evolving and changing.

Everything we all hope for in life is perfection, but in reality nothing is perfect, we can only get very close to perfection in all experience because what is right and works now, looking very good today may not be that way tomorrow.

Looking for perfection in life can be very daunting, but adjusting to everything around you can make the journey of school run interesting, by resonating in your mind daily that nothing is perfect, but one can only work towards it. *"A little patience with an open mind in that challenging job can lead to a rewarding career."*

FINDING JOY IN SCHOOL RUNS

You can turn your trials into triumphs if only you can turn your thoughts to positive and be happy. No moment in life is perfect, your willingness to grow into your highest potential will only align to what you are here to do in life.

School runs is just like any other work, if you don't develop a genuine interest in anything you are doing and you are doing it grudgingly, at the end of the day it is just like imprisonment for you. Many of us wait for the perfect moment and opportunity but there is not any perfect moment. Nothing and no one are perfect.

The interest you put in school runs will put unquantifiable quality into how your children turn out at the end of the day and the happiness this brings into your mind and your life. We are all meant to enjoy life and be happy because life is to be enjoyed, not the other way around. More so, any work that brings out happiness in life, brings fulfilment. **Those things that will define you are things that are often reflected in your children's achievements**.

Accomplishments in your children's educational life has a bearing on your dreams and your dream for them, and it is extremely exciting when you genuinely believe in what you are doing and how this eventually pays off.

"The lesson learnt here is about enduring what life brings along with a positive disposition that will eventually leads to a success story."

13. CONFIDENCE ABOUT TOMMORROW

Confidence emanates from the mind. Whatever the mind can conceive or believe, can then be easily achieved because tomorrow always comes whether we like it or not. Seeing yourself or visualizing yourself today in the best possible way is key to doing school runs with joy which speaks volumes.

Perceiving and projecting yourself in a positive and elegant way would boost your everyday confidence without being vain or overbearing. It is all about your mindset. If you struggle with low self-confidence because of memories of certain challenges you have encountered before, then you will struggle to enjoy school runs at any point in time. Therefore, always avoid putting yourself down during such periods of juggling with your daily routine.

"Achieving your goals in life should not be affected by school visits". Genuinely practicing perceiving yourself as an eventual

success is not a delusion but a positive projection of a reality that is possible, and which would eventually materialize if one is focused enough and work towards it.

Challenges in life can easily deflate you, but the most important thing in life to remember that such events are part and parcel of life's developmental process. In such periods, you must learn to accommodate, manage, and navigate your way around it all to gain the much-desired outcome. No matter what you face in life, always maintain a positive outlook which ultimately becomes a powerful tool not only in your daily school visits activity but also in other areas of your life.

14. SCHOOL RUNS SELF-AUDIT QUESTIONEER

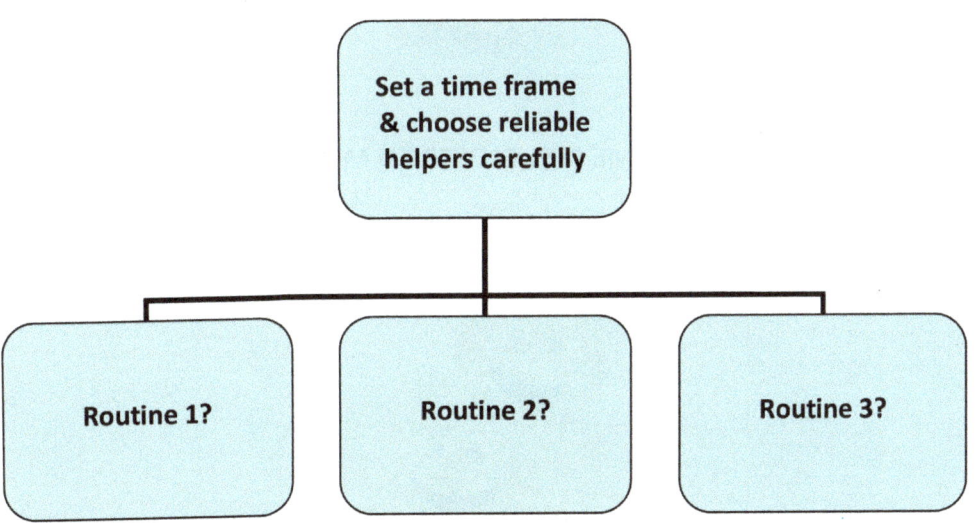

HOW DO YOU FEEL ABOUT SCHOOL RUN?

- UTTERLY TEDIOUS??

FINDING JOY IN SCHOOL RUNS

- **IT MAKES ME FEEL CLOSER TO MY CHILDREN??**

- **I DON'T AND WON'T DO IT**

14. SCHOOL RUNS SELF-AUDIT QUESTIONEER

DESCRIBE YOU WILL LIKE SCHOOL RUN TO

- JOINING IT YOURSELF
- GET SOMEONE/NANNY TO DO IT FOR YOU
- TAKE WITH OTHER FRIENDS/PARENTS EITHER WEEKLY, FORTNIGHTLY OR MONTHLY
- TAKE WITH YOUR PARTNER/HUSBAND

WHO SHOULD BE DOING SCHOOL RUN ROUTINE?

- MUM
- DAD (WHY)??
- MUM (WHY)??
- DAD
- GET A NANNY

FINDING JOY IN SCHOOL RUNS

HOW CAN YOU ENJOY SCHOOL AND BE DEPRESSED?

- DAILY ACTIVITIES TO LOOK FORWARD TO THE CHILDREN
- MAKE THE DAY FUN ON A DAILY BASIS
- CONNECTING WITH YOUR CHILDREN BY STUFF/ BAKING/ MAKING DISHES/SHOPPING OR RELAX TOGETHER

DAILY ROUTINE ACTIVITIES AFTER DROP OFFF AND PICKING ON DAILY OR WEEKLY

- DO YOU HAVE A PLAN B IN CASE OF UNFORESEEN CIRCUMSTANCES?
- PLAN B TO AVOID BEEN STRESSED
- FLEXIBILITY WITH YOUR TIME FOR SCHOOL RUN AND 2 TWO FOR NANNY OR HELP

LIST OF ACTIVITIES OF INTEREST TO ENGAGE IN BEFORE PICK UP TIME.

- EDUCATIONAL SHORT COURSES, MOTIVATIONAL SPEAKING, SEMINARS, EXHIBITIONS
- SPORTS ACTIVITY
- CREATIVE ACIVITIES
- CAREER IMPROVEMENT

14. SCHOOL RUNS SELF-AUDIT QUESTIONEER

- BUSINESS IDEAS TO GENERATE INCOME

- BE YOUR OWN BOSS

- DEVELOP YOUR CREATIVE IDEAS

- PART TIME JOB OPPORTUNITY

- HAVE A PLAN B IN PLACE IN CASE YOU ARE RUNNING LATE TO PICK UP INORDER TO AVOID STRESS

"SCHOOL RUNS IS FUN AND CAN BE A THING OF JOY IF YOU PUT YOUR MIND TO IT."

Lightning Source UK Ltd.
Milton Keynes UK
UKHW052013120720
366413UK00007B/46